Miley Cyrus

ABDO
Publishing Company

A Big Buddy Book
by **Sarah Tieck**

VISIT US AT
www.abdopublishing.com

Published by ABDO Publishing Company, 8000 West 78th Street, Edina, Minnesota 55439.

Copyright © 2009 by Abdo Consulting Group, Inc. International copyrights reserved in all countries. No part of this book may be reproduced in any form without written permission from the publisher. Buddy Books™ is a trademark and logo of ABDO Publishing Company.

Printed in the United States.

Coordinating Series Editor: Rochelle Baltzer
Contributing Editors: Heidi M.D. Elston, Megan M. Gunderson, Marcia Zappa
Graphic Design: Maria Hosley
Cover Photograph: AP Photo: Kevork Djansezian
Interior Photographs/Illustrations: AP Photo: Mary Altaffer (page 5), Tammie Arroyo (page 7), Worcester Telegram and Gazette, Ed Collier (page 29), Damian Dovarganes (page 5), Jennifer Graylock (pages 15, 23), Boys and Girls Club of America/John Hayes (page 16), Gary He (page 27), Mark Humphrey (page 11), Robert E. Klein (page 27), Danny Moloshok (page 20), Amanda Parks (page 25), Chris Pizzello (page 18), AP Images for Fox/Matt Sayles (page 19); Getty Images: John Chlasson/Liason (page 11), Ron Galella/Ltd/WireImage (page 8); Photos.com: (page 13).

Library of Congress Cataloging-in-Publication Data

Tieck, Sarah, 1976-
  Miley Cyrus / Sarah Tieck.
    p. cm. -- (Big buddy biographies)
  Includes index.
  ISBN 978-1-60453-119-0
  1. Cyrus, Miley, 1992---Juvenile literature. 2. Singers--United States--Biography--Juvenile literature. 3. Actresses--United States--Biography--Juvenile literature. I. Title.

  ML3930.C98T54 2008
  782.42164092--dc22
  [B]
                          2008010465

Contents

An Overnight Sensation

Miley Cyrus is a famous teenager. She is a singer and an actress. Miley is best known as the star of *Hannah Montana*.

Hannah Montana is a popular television show. It **debuted** March 24, 2006, on the Disney Channel. Since then, the show has gained millions of fans around the world. Now, fans can buy Hannah Montana products and albums or attend concerts.

Hannah Montana is about a normal girl named Miley Stewart who has a secret. She is also a famous pop star named Hannah Montana! To hide who she is, Miley Stewart wears a blonde wig to play Hannah Montana.

Family Ties

Miley Ray Cyrus was born on November 23, 1992, in Franklin, Tennessee. Her parents are Billy Ray and Leticia "Tish" Cyrus.

Miley has five **siblings**. Her older brothers are Christopher Cody and Trace. Miley's older sister is Brandi. Her younger brother is Braison, and her younger sister is Noah.

On *Hannah Montana*, Miley Stewart's mother is dead and her father raises her. Many fans think Miley Cyrus's life is the same. But, both Billy Ray and Tish play an active part in Miley's life.

The Cyrus family is very close. Tish, Billy Ray, Braison, and other family members often attend events with Miley.

Miley's name used to be Destiny Hope Cyrus. As a child, she received the nickname "Smiley." Over time, that was shortened to Miley. That name stuck. In 2008, she legally changed her name to Miley Ray Cyrus.

Miley's parents chose the name Destiny Hope because they thought their daughter was destined to do great things.

Word of Mouth

The year Miley was born, her dad had a hit song! Billy Ray's catchy country tune is called "Achy Breaky Heart." It made Billy Ray famous. The song also sparked people's interest in **line dancing**!

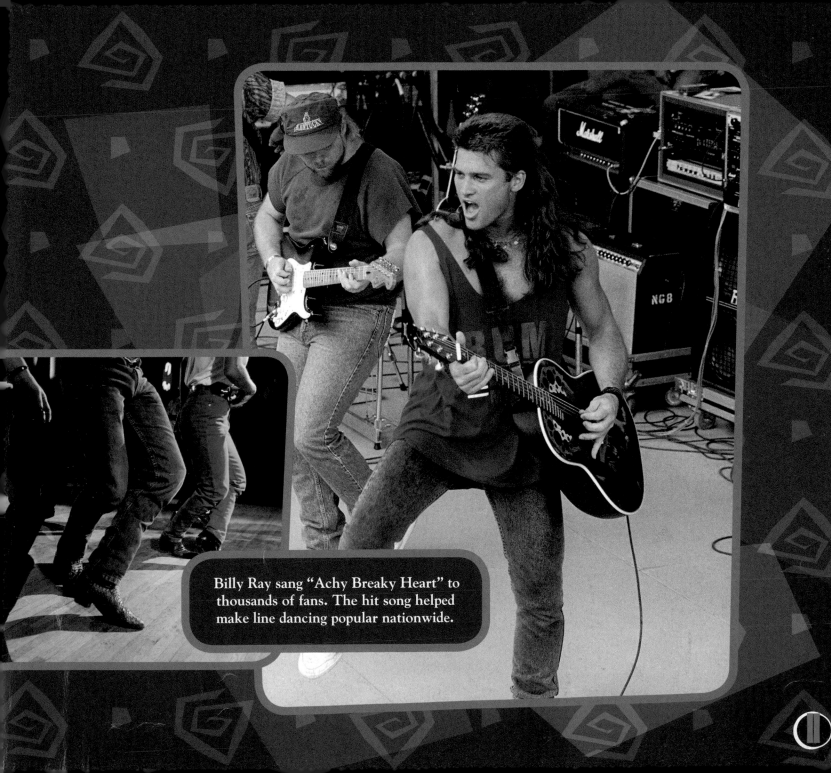

Billy Ray sang "Achy Breaky Heart" to thousands of fans. The hit song helped make line dancing popular nationwide.

Country Life

Even though her dad was a country music star, Miley had a quiet childhood. She grew up on her family's 500-acre (200-ha) farm in Franklin, Tennessee. It is near the state capital, Nashville.

Miley's country roots show through when she talks. Like many people from Tennessee, she has a slight southern **accent**.

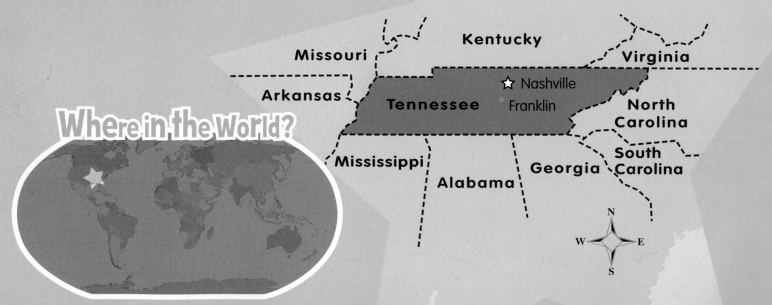

Where in the World?

Did you know...

Miley's godmother is famous country singer Dolly Parton. On *Hannah Montana*, Dolly plays the role of Miley Stewart's aunt.

At their Tennessee farm, the Cyruses spend time outside. They take care of animals such as dogs, horses, and chickens.

After becoming an actress and a singer, Miley left school. Instead, she worked with a tutor. Having a private teacher made it possible for her to travel and perform.

Miley spent her childhood in the small town of Franklin. She attended classes at Heritage Middle School. She also went to church with her family.

A Rising Star

Miley decided to follow in her dad's show business footsteps. She became an actress when she was just nine years old!

However, Miley wasn't always famous. When she started out, she had small parts in television shows and movies.

Because of their work, Miley and Billy Ray spend a lot of time together. Talks in the car and time on stage and on set keep them close.

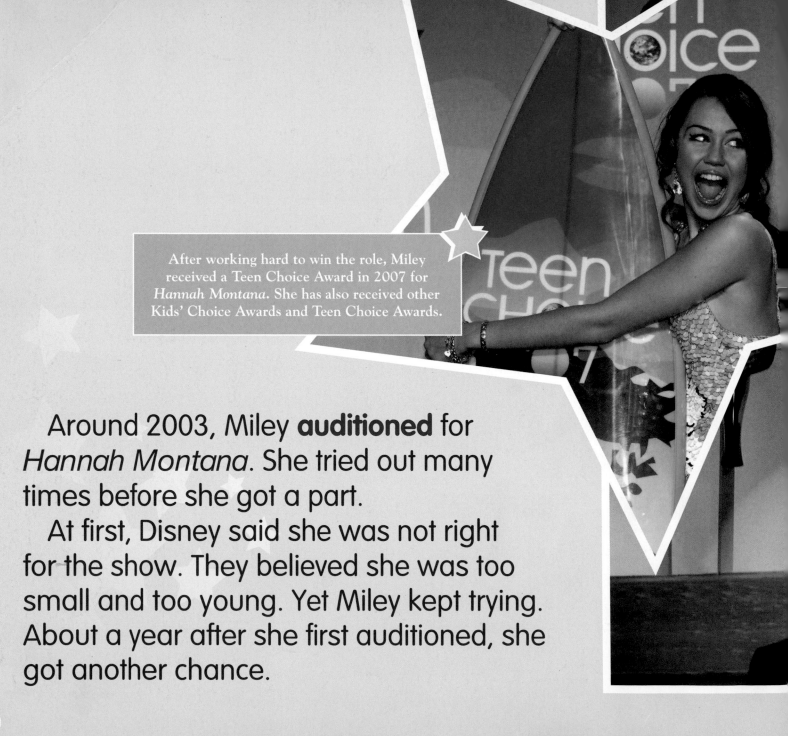

After working hard to win the role, Miley received a Teen Choice Award in 2007 for *Hannah Montana*. She has also received other Kids' Choice Awards and Teen Choice Awards.

Around 2003, Miley **auditioned** for *Hannah Montana*. She tried out many times before she got a part.

At first, Disney said she was not right for the show. They believed she was too small and too young. Yet Miley kept trying. About a year after she first auditioned, she got another chance.

Miley presented one of the 2007 Teen Choice Awards with the Jonas Brothers. Award winners receive special surfboards.

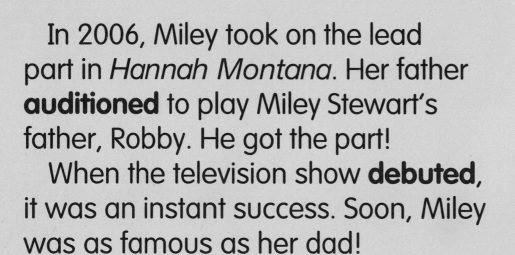

In 2006, Miley took on the lead part in *Hannah Montana*. Her father **auditioned** to play Miley Stewart's father, Robby. He got the part!

When the television show **debuted**, it was an instant success. Soon, Miley was as famous as her dad!

Hannah Montana turned out to be Miley's big break. The show has millions of fans!

Dreams Come True

After starting work on *Hannah Montana*, Miley appeared in popular magazines and on television. She has been in *People* magazine many times. And in 2007, Miley was a guest on *The Oprah Winfrey Show*.

Today, fans can purchase Hannah Montana clothes, toys, albums, and DVDs. The albums even include songs Miley wrote!

Good Friends

Miley's good friends are part of the *Hannah Montana* cast. She is close to Emily Osment, the actress who plays Lilly.

Off the set, Miley taught Emily to play guitar. And, Emily showed Miley how to knit. Sometimes, these friends are too busy to hang out. So, they send text messages and call each other.

Mitchel Musso, Billy Ray Cyrus, Miley Cyrus, Emily Osment, and Jason Earles star in *Hannah Montana*.

Joe, Kevin, and Nick Jonas of the Jonas Brothers toured with Miley Cyrus.

On the Road

In 2007, Miley traveled North America for the Best of Both Worlds concert tour. She sang some songs as herself and others as Hannah Montana.

All of the concerts sold out quickly. The tour was so popular that more concerts were added in 2008.

In 2008, a film version of the Best of Both Worlds concerts appeared in theaters. It was a hit with fans.

Buzz

Miley agreed to live with her parents until she turns 20. They plan to create a special part of the house just for her. Miley has a bright **future**. She plans to continue acting and making music. A *Hannah Montana* movie is being planned. It is expected to be in theaters in 2008 or 2009. Miley is also working on a book about her life. It is due out in 2009. Fans have high hopes for rising star Miley Cyrus.

Miley wrote many of the songs on the album *Hannah Montana 2: Meet Miley Cyrus*. She continues to write songs for future albums.

Snapshot

★ **Name**: Miley Ray Cyrus

★ **Birthday**: November 23, 1992

★ **Birthplace**: Franklin, Tennessee

★ **Homes**: Los Angeles, California and Franklin, Tennessee

★ **Appearances**: *Doc*, "If Heartaches Had Wings," *Big Fish*, *Hannah Montana*

★ **Toured with**: The Jonas Brothers

Important Words

accent a special way of saying words or phrases used by people from certain areas or countries.

audition (aw-DIH-shuhn) to give a trial performance showcasing personal talent as a musician, a singer, a dancer, or an actor.

debut (DAY-byoo) a first appearance.

future (FYOO-chuhr) a time that has not yet occurred.

guitar (guh-TAHR) a stringed musical instrument played by strumming.

knit (NIHT) to make fabric by connecting yarn with a series of loops.

legal based on or allowed by law.

line dance a dance in which people move together in a line.

nickname a name that replaces a person's real name.

sibling a brother or a sister.

Web Sites

To learn more about Miley Cyrus, visit ABDO Publishing Company on the World Wide Web. Web sites about Miley Cyrus are featured on our Book Links page. These links are routinely monitored and updated to provide the most current information available.

www.abdopublishing.com

Index